THIS BOOK IS
A JOKE

Other books, some of them by Holly Kowitt:

Nuclear Physics Made Difficult
101 Broccoli Jokes
A Scrunchie for Caitlin
Totally Truman! The Story of a Presidential Hottie
The Complete Works of William Shakespeare

# THIS BOOK IS
## A JOKE

### BY HOLLY KOWITT

SCHOLASTIC INC.
New York   Toronto   London   Auckland   Sydney   Mexico City
New Delhi   Hong Kong   Buenos Aires

ISBN 0-439-67171-X
Copyright © 2004 by Holly Kowitt. All rights reserved. Published by Scholastic Inc., 557 Broadway, New York, NY 10012.
SCHOLASTIC and associated logos are trademarks and/or registered trademarks of Scholastic Inc.

12 11 10 9 8 7 6 5 4 3                                    5 6 7 8 9/0

Printed in the U.S.A.
First printing, November 2004

*To me, whose selfless hard work
and never-ending ideas
made this book possible.*

## Acknowledgments

I'd like to thank Jeanne Heifetz,
David Manis, Mort Milder,
Ellen Miles, Brawler, Sand Razor,
and Night Attack Chopper. Some of
these are names of G.I. JOE
attack vehicles.

# STAFF LIST

WITH THANKS TO MY DEVOTED STAFF . . .

| | |
|---|---|
| EDITOR IN CHIEF | U. DE MANN |
| PROOFREADER | DIANA BOREDOM |
| COPY EDITOR | MANNY ERRORS |
| FACT-CHECKER | MISS TAKES |
| TECH SUPPORT | C. MANUAL |
| ASSISTANT WRITER | PHILIP SPACE |
| ILLUSTRATOR | DREW STUFF |
| KNOCK-KNOCK CONSULTANT | HUGHES THERE |
| INSULT EDITOR | JOE MAMA |
| PERSONAL TRAINER | JIM SHORTZ |
| DRIVER | RUSTY VANN |
| CHEF | MAC DONALDS |
| EDITOR OF THE SEQUEL | XAVIER MONEY |

# FOREWORD

The book you are reading is the result of *several hours* of work. It weighs in at over *two ounces* and is a *quarter inch thick.* Laid side by side, the pages would reach *from one end of your bed to the other!*

A work this impressive begs the question: *How does she do it?* It's not easy to come up with another pig joke, or a list of cannibal pickup lines. And it takes time — time that could be better spent playing air hockey or online shopping.

Being a joke writer is a lonely job. But when I think of all the kids out there who need me, I just have to sit down and write one more vomit joke. It's the thought of YOU, desperate to avoid homework, that keeps me going.

Holly "Holly" Kowitt

# MY HOMEWORK ATE MY DOG

## School Jokes

We think these jokes are pretty classy. Then again, we have no principals.

What happened when the teacher tied all the students' shoelaces together?
They went on a class trip.

Teacher: What do you call someone who keeps talking when people are no longer interested?
Student: A teacher?

What's a mall rat's favorite subject?
Buy-ology.

What do George Washington, Abraham Lincoln, and Christopher Columbus have in common?
They were all born on a holiday.

# HOT NUMBERS

Where do algebra teachers soak after a long, hard day?
The math tub.

Who did the math teacher date?
A real hot number.

What do you serve a math teacher for dessert?
Pi.

Where do math teachers eat?
The lunch counter.

Why did the math teacher cry on the last day of school?
He hates to be divided from his class.

Why did the teacher jump in the lake?
She wanted to test the waters.

Teacher: Why did you copy Danny's test?
Jimmy: What gave me away?
Teacher: His name on your paper.

What happened to the cannibal who ate his teacher?
He had to cook with substitutes.

Teacher: Will you two stop interrupting class by trading cards?
Jimmy: We're not trading cards, we're playing video games.

Band student: Our school played the Beatles last night!
Gym student: Who won?

Teacher: You missed school yesterday, didn't you?
Debby: No — I didn't miss it at all!

Teacher: What do you know about the Dead Sea?
Peter: I didn't even know it was sick!

Why was the music teacher angry?
The kids were always passing notes.

 # TOP TEN BEST HOMEWORK EXCUSES

1. I didn't have time — my sister needed my kidney.
2. I converted to a religion that forbids algebra.
3. We had to use it for toilet paper when our plane went down in the desert.

4. My brother sold it on eBay.
5. It was confiscated for national security reasons. I can't say any more.
6. My imaginary friend borrowed it and never gave it back.
7. I threw it at someone who said you *weren't* the best teacher in school.
8. Shaq was sick, so the Lakers asked me to fill in.
9. It was due May 12th of *this* year? Dang!
10. I don't remember anything after the aliens landed.

Teacher: Who started this fight?

Jason: Peter threw a spitball at me, so I threw one back.

Teacher: Why didn't you come get me?

Jason: 'Cause your aim is lousy.


Why did the teacher marry the janitor?

He swept her off her feet.


What book was King Arthur read as a baby?

*Good Knight Moon.*

## DIFFERENT KINDS OF SCHOOL

What kind of school do you go to if you are . . .

. . . an ice-cream man?

Sundae school

. . . a surfer?

Boarding school

. . . a giant?

High school

. . . King Arthur?

Knight school

KNIGHT
SCHOOL

Bobby: I can't figure out this math problem.
Teacher: Really? Any five-year-old should get it.
Bobby: No wonder—I'm nine.

Teacher: Where is the English Channel?
David: I don't know. We don't have cable.

Zachary dawdled on his way to school. "Hurry up!" said his mom. "You'll be late!"
"What's the rush?" Zachary asked. "They're open till 3:30."

Teacher: Jimmy, I hope I didn't see you copying Amy's test paper.
Jimmy: Boy, I hope you didn't either!

Why did the student bring scissors to school?
He wanted to cut class.

Teacher: I was very pleased to give you an 85 on the test.
Student: Why don't you give me 100 and really enjoy yourself?

Teacher: Please don't hum while you're working.
Student: I'm not working — I'm just humming.

Father: Why are you home from school so late?
Jeff: I was the only one who could answer a question.
Father: Really? What was the question?
Jeff: Who threw a spitball at the teacher?

Who are the most popular boys in school?
Art and Gym.

Andy: Hey, Mom, tomorrow there's a small PTA meeting.
Mother: What do you mean by small?
Andy: You, me, and the principal.

Father: You've got 4 D's and a C on this report card.
Randy: Maybe I concentrated too much on one subject.

Craig: I don't think my teacher likes me.
Jimmy: Why do you say that?
Craig: During fire drills he tells me to stay seated.

Teacher: At your age I could name all the presidents.
Student: Yeah, but back then there were only three of them.

Teacher: What family does the aardvark belong to?
Student: I don't know any family who has one.

Teacher: When Eskimos used to trade, they used fish instead of money.
Student: They must have had a hard time getting candy bars from a vending machine.


Teacher: Why didn't you answer the question, "Who shot Lincoln?"
Student: Hey — I'm no squealer.


Jane: I know someone who's thirty-five and still in fourth grade.
Billy: No way.
Jane: *Way!* She's my teacher.


Teacher: Luke, were you copying the answer from your neighbor's paper?
Luke: No, just checking to see if she had mine right.


What does a lady principal wear under her clothes?
A permission slip.


Why did the kid bring his dad's charge card to class?
He wanted the extra credit.


Jill: Want to go to the mall after school?
Lil: Can't. I have to help my dad with my homework.

Dad, will you do my homework for me?
Sorry, son, it just wouldn't be right.
Yeah, but you could *try.*


Bob and Rob turned in their quizzes at the same time. When they got their tests back, they both got fourteen out of fifteen answers right. Their teacher talked to them afterward.
Teacher: You both missed number fifteen, but Bob is going to pass the course, and Rob will have to stay behind.
Rob: But if we both missed the same question, why are you passing him?
Teacher: Because he answered the question "I don't know" and you answered it "Neither do I."


Librarian: We've discovered an overdue book you've had for some time now.
Student: Do I owe a big fine?
Librarian: Let's put it this way, the new wing will be named after you.


David was good at forging signatures — so good that he started charging friends to write their absentee notes. One day the teacher found out. "Well, David," said the teacher. "You'd better have a good excuse for me."
"I do," said David. "But it'll cost you."


Teacher: Ryan, use the word *odyssey* in a sentence.
Ryan: You *odyssey* the new Star Wars!
Teacher: No, no. Try the word *gladiator.*
Ryan: A monster ate my sister and I'm *gladiator.*
Teacher: Good grief. I'll give you one more chance. Use the word *handsome* in a sentence.
Ryan: *Handsome* gum over, will ya?

Knock knock.
Who's there?
Diploma.
Diploma who?
Diploma's coming to fix de sink.


Knock knock.
Who's there?
Locker.
Locker who?
Locker in the closet if you find her!

# AT THE ALL-STATE DINER

Georgia: Ohio!

Cal: Hey, Hawaii you?

Georgia: So, Mr. Sippi, where's Mississippi? Can she join us?

Cal: She's Washington of laundry right now—Alaska. Are you thirsty? We have Kansas of Coke.

Georgia: Just a Minnesota for me. What happened to the chicken bone Diana swallowed?

Cal: Still Indiana. And how's your Maine man?

Georgia: He annoys me, Illinois you. Missouri loves company.

Cal: Utah can't agree on anything. How was the party? Did Delaware her New Jersey?

Georgia: I didn't see, but Arkansas. What are you up to later?

Cal: I thought Idaho my Maryland, or pay my Texas.

Georgia: Thanks for the drink. Iowa you a dollar.

Cal: Wyoming any money? It's on me!

# HOMESCHOOLING:
## The Pros and Cons

**PRO** Relaxed dress code

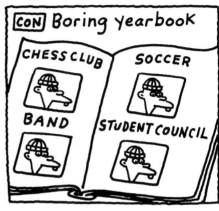

**CON** Boring yearbook

CHESS CLUB

SOCCER

BAND

STUDENT COUNCIL

**PRO** No more idiotic roles in the school play

**CON** Lousy fire drills

Form a single file line, People!

**PRO** You're a shoo-in for class president.

THANK YOU! THANK YOU!

VOTE 4 ME

**CON** Low attendance at school dances

This stinks.

# THE EIGHT TYPES

## The Airhead

**"Is this outfit too matchy-matchy?"**

**Fave activities: Shopping, best friend collages**
**Dream job: Lip gloss tester**
**Overheard: "I think, therefore I. M."**

## The Geek

**"Not to bring up *Star Wars* again, but . . ."**

**Fave activities: Insect Club, Mathmaniacs**
**Dream job: Captain, *Starship Enterprise***
**Overheard: "You! Off my planet!"**

## The Idiot

"Well, um, er, huh?"

**Fave activity: Burping the alphabet**
**Dream job: Video game tester**
**Overheard: "Ratman #87 will be**
**worth a lot someday."**

## The Goody-Goody

"Hey! You forgot to collect our homework!"

**Fave activity: Kissing up to teachers**
**Dream job: IRS auditor**
**Overheard: "More brownies, Mr. Loomis?"**

# THE EIGHT TYPES

## The Playa

"I'm just using this scooter till I get my Benz."

**Fave activity: Chillin', illin'**
**Dream job: Jillionaire**
**Overheard: "For the last time,**
**my name isn't *Bernie*!"**

## The Diva

"I wish *I* could date me!"

**Fave activities: Strutting, stylin',**
**and more strutting**
**Dream job: Karaoke star**
**Overheard: "Would the world be better if**
**there were *three* of me?"**

## Girl from Mars

**"Is it just me, or does soap taste delicious?"**

**Fave activities: Paper clip
sculpture, vegan poetry
Dream job: UFO flight attendant
Overheard: "Allow me to
introduce myselves."**

## The Foreign Exchange Student

**"Catch you on the rebound!"**

**Fave activities: Yodeling, yo-yoing
Dream job: Sauerkraut farmer
Overheard: "Don't have an ox!"**

# THINGS YOU DON'T WANT TO HEAR
## in the School Cafeteria

Hey, Betty- Someone finally chose the devilled broccoli!

If you find a nail clipper in there, it's mine!

Your dad isn't a health inspector, is he?

It's _probably_ mayonnaise.

I'm not sure how old the chili squares are. I've only worked here a month.

Yes, Dr. Lecter, we _do_ have a job opening!

Hey-I found the Kindergarten turtle!

EEEEEEEEEEEKK!!!

# THINGS YOU DON'T WANT TO SEE
## in the School Cafeteria

# INSIDE THE

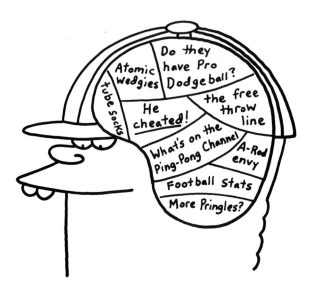

The Jock

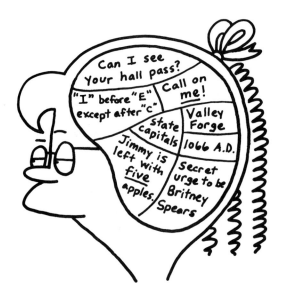

The "A" Student

# MIND OF . . .

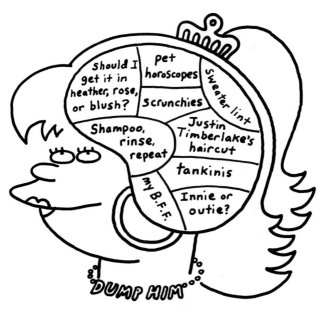

The Mall Rat

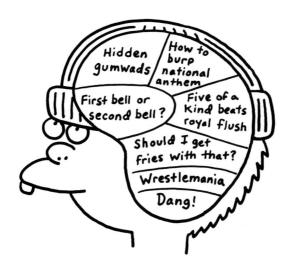

The "D" Student

# I DON'T WANT TO BOA YOU

## Animal Jokes

We think you'll really gopher these, and we're not lion.

Where do birds invest their money?
The stork market.

Why did the teacher bring birdseed to her meeting?
It was a parrot–teacher conference.

What's a bird's favorite motto?
"If at first you don't succeed, fly, fly again."

Why did the bird sing after dinner?
He wanted more tweet.

What has feathers and writes?
A ballpoint hen.

Why did the hen bring her baby to the grocery store?
She wanted to pay by chick.


Why did the dog run out to the yard?
He got an urgent bone call.


**What did the chick say at the rap concert?**
**"I wanna give a shout-out to my peeps. . . ."**

Whadaya say to a chicken in a beauty contest?
Lotsa cluck.


What has leather, feathers, and rides a Harley?
A biker chick.


When a pig's in trouble, what number does he call?
Swine-one-one.

Why did the pig throw his exam in the mud?
It was a plop quiz.

Why did the pig help the old lady cross the street?
He wanted to join the Boy Snouts.

Why did the pig turn down a party invitation?
He wasn't in the mud.

What's every pig's favorite game?
Wallow the Leader.

What do you get when pigs learn karate?
Pork chops.

What does a pig do in the fall?
His back-to-school slopping.

Two cows are in a barn. One says to the other, "So, what do you think about mad cow disease?"
The other says, "What do I care? I'm a helicopter."

What beauty pageant did the cow win?
The Moos America Contest.

Why do cows make good basketball players?
They've got all the right hooves.

What does a cow carry to work?
His beef case.

Why didn't the calf get chosen for the football team?
He didn't make the cutlet.

Why did the dog go to the museum?
He heard there was free barking.

Why did the mouse crawl under the dog?
He wanted a woof over his head.

How did the dog stop the VCR tape?
He hit the paws button.

How is a dog like a telephone?
They both have collar ID.

Why did the dog sleep under the car?
Because he wanted to get up oily in the morning.

What kind of exam do you give a dog?
A pup quiz.

First mailman: A dog bit me on the leg this morning!
Second mailman: Did you put anything on it?
First mailman: No, he liked it plain!

What does a kitten say when it wins an Oscar®?
"I'd like to thank the members of the A-cat-emy. . . ."

When Daddy Buffalo leaves for work, what does he say to his little boy?
"Bye, son."

What kind of bears like to go out in the rain?
Drizzly bears.

Two grizzly bears were strolling through Times Square. One turned to the other and said, "Not many people around today, are there?"

What's a skunk's favorite snack?
Stench fries.

What do you call a skunk with ESP?
A fortune smeller.

What do you get when a tortoise blocks the sun?
A turtle eclipse.

How do turtles get to the second floor?
They take the shell-evator.

Why couldn't the monkey phone the king of the jungle?
Because the lion was busy.

What part of school do tigers like best?
Lunge time.


Why did the leopard go to the cleaners?
His coat was covered with spots.


Why did the rabbit go on strike?
He wanted a better celery.

How did the skunk call home?
On his smell phone.

What's the first thing a rabbit reads in the newspaper?
Lettuce to the editor.

What do beavers do for fun on weekend nights?
Hold a lumber party.

What do you say to a rodent entering a relay race?
"You *go,* squirrel!"

What sign did they hang over the ape house?
"Satisfaction guaranteed or double your monkey back."

Why can't leopards become undercover agents?
Because they're always spotted.

What's a cat's favorite dinner?
Spaghetti and hairballs.

What's the best way to revive a dying rodent?
Mouse-to-mouse resuscitation!

Where do otters come from?
Otter space.

Why didn't the letter get delivered to the frog?
It had the wrong zip toad.

What do you say when a frog orders a hamburger?
"Would you like flies with that?"

Where can you see your favorite frog band?
*Toad-al Request Live.*

What do frogs do when they play basketball?
They take jump shots.

What happened when the frog parked his car in front of a fire hydrant?
It was toad!

Why did the lobster study so hard?
He wanted to go to claw school.

Why was the young whale sent to the principal?
He was always spouting off at the teacher.

How does a fish pay his bills?
With a credit cod.

What did the dolphin's computer say?
"You've got whale!"

What did the fish wear when she got married?
A wetting dress.

What happened to the sardine who didn't show up for work?
He was canned.

How do sharks like their steak?
Whale-done.

A man walked into the doctor's office with an aardvark on his head. "You need help right away!" exclaimed the doctor.
"I certainly do!" said the aardvark. "Could you get this man out from under me?"

A guy walks into a diner and sees a horse working behind the counter. The guy can't stop staring, which prompts the horse to ask, "What's wrong? You've never seen a horse serving coffee before?"
"It's not that," said the guy. "I just never thought the bear would sell this place."

Three hunters walking in the woods came upon strange tracks. The first hunter said, "These are moose tracks."
The second said, "No, these are bear tracks."
The third never got to say anything because he was hit by a train.

John was walking his dog near the lake when a duck walked by and shouted, "Hi!"
John was so startled he said, "Wow! I didn't know ducks could talk!"
"Neither did I!" exclaimed the dog.

A man went to the vet to collect his sick dog. The vet came in carrying the dog and said, "I'm really sorry, but I'm going to have to put your dog down."
The man burst into tears. "Why?"
"Because he's too heavy."

On top of a burning building, a woman held her pet cat in her arms.
"Throw the cat down!" yelled a man below.
"I'm afraid you'll drop him!" she shouted back.
"Don't worry," he said. "I'm a professional soccer player."
The woman carefully dropped the cat off the roof. The athlete made a fantastic catch, then bounced the cat three times on his head and kicked it over a wall.

Bob: Last week I was thrown out of the zoo for feeding the monkeys.
Rob: What's so bad about that?
Bob: I fed them to the lions.

Ben: This is my pet chimp. Is it okay if I keep him in our locker during class?
Ken: What about the smell?
Ben: Oh, he'll get used to it!

A woman walked into a pet shop and said, "I'd like a rabbit for my son."
"Sorry, ma'am," said the pet shop owner. "We don't do exchanges."

A lion woke up one morning with the urge to flaunt power over his fellow beasts. So he went over to a monkey and roared, "Who is the mightiest animal in the jungle?"

"You are," said the monkey, shaking.

Then the lion came across a parrot.

"Who is the mightiest animal in the jungle?" roared the lion.

"You are, master," said the parrot, swallowing in fear.

Next, the lion met an elephant.

"Who is the mightiest animal in the jungle?" roared the lion.

The elephant grabbed the lion with his trunk, turned him upside down, and then dropped him on his head and shuffled off.

"All right," the lion shouted after him. "There's no need to be nasty just because you don't know the answer!"

Knock knock.
Who's there?
Halibut.
Halibut who?
Halibut a kiss, dear?


Knock knock.
Who's there?
Buzzard.
Buzzard who?
Buzzard doesn't work, so I had to knock!


Knock knock.
Who's there?
Fido.
Fido who?
Fido known you were coming, I'd have baked a cake!


Knock knock.
Who's there?
Aardvark.
Aardvark who?
Aardvark a mile for one of your smiles.


Knock knock.
Who's there?
The owl says.
The owl says who?
Exactly.

# RHINO YOU ARE, BUT WHAT AM I?

See if you can lick this animal quiz.

True or False:

1. When vultures fly, they're allowed two carrion bags.
2. A flamingo stands on one leg because it lost a shoe.
3. Gorillas have large nostrils because they have big fingers.

Choose the right answer.

4. **Insects have antennae because they** _____
   a) need them to taste and smell.
   b) can't afford cable.
   c) get confused because their uncles are ants.

5. **Single-cell animals are** _____
   a) the simplest animals.
   b) animals with only one cell phone.
   c) always saying they've got to "split."

6. **Chameleons are known for changing** _____
   a) colors.
   b) hairstyles.
   c) long-distance companies.

7. **Frogs don't drink because** _____
   a) they take in water through their skin.
   b) they're all out of Diet Croak.
   c) they're *toad-ally* not thirsty.

8. **The Komodo dragon is a massive reptile that's looking for** _____
   a) water buffalo.
   b) lost contact lenses.
   c) more rock, less talk.

**9. Anacondas have been known to swallow _____ in a single gulp.**
a) a whole deer
b) their pride
c) a Snake 'n' Bake dinner

**10. Tortoises retreat into their shell because _____**
a) they need protection from predators.
b) there's no business like slow business.
c) they want to watch *Turtle Request Live.*

**11. Sharks let the remora fish travel on their backs because _____**
a) they eat parasites off the sharks' skin.
b) they like saying, "Dinner's on me tonight!"
c) together they can watch *America's Moist Wanted.*

**12. During the winter, most birds _____**
a) migrate south to their winter homes.
b) open branch offices.
c) stay home and watch the Feather Channel.

**13. I bought this book because I _____**
a) had $5.99 to throw away.
b) needed a coaster for giant soft drinks.
c) thought it would make an easy book report.

**ANSWERS:**
1. F 2. F 3. F Questions 1–3: Give yourself one point for each false answer. Questions 4–13: Give yourself two points for every question you answered "a."

**SCORING:**
23 points — Purr-fect
11 points or more — Sow-sow
10 points or less — Beastly

# I'd Like to Get to Gnaw You

## Animal Personal Ads

King of the jungle, tired of lion around, wants to be your mane man. If you like to hunt, I'm game. Or we could just go to the maul. No cheetahs. Larry@earthlynx.edu.

Dinosaur seeks date to step out on the town. Sixty million years old but looks fifty million, looking for someone to stalk to. Don't keep me wading! 555-TREX.

Cobra, very striking, seeks main squeeze. Looking for someone with a charming poisonality. 555-HISS.

I'll lay it on the line: Good-looking hen, tired of cheep guys, likes romance, adventure, and dancing chick-to-chick. Don't answer if you're my eggs-husband. S.Cooper@feather.net.

Where are all the edible bachelors? Black widow spider would like to get to gnaw you. I like guys — especially with hot sauce. 555-LEGS.

Peacock with gorgeous blue and green feathers, a shiny red chest, long silver neck, and sturdy legs. Actually, I'm not looking for anyone, I just like to talk about myself!

Ape seeks the gorilla of my dreams. Very buff from working out in jungle gym. What sign were you born under? Mine said, Do Not Feed the Monkeys. Tree-mail me at Harry@hair.net.

Laboratory retriever, a real rabies man, seeks fetching companion. Join me for some old sneakers and water from the toilet bowl. Flea-mail: Fido@drooler.edu.

Cow, out standing in my field, Ox-ford educated, not easily suede. I love mooseums, moovies, moosic, and won't keep you out pasture bed-time. Let's meat. Gus@hay-ol.com.

Skunk seeks independent mate who can stink for herself. Will you be the scenter of my world? Call me on my smell. 555-7294.

# THE PATIENT IS A LITTLE HOARSE

Here are some animal medical records we fetched.

Patient: Squirrel
Notes: Completely flattened. Patient has that "rundown" feeling.
Diagnosis: Seems like a real nutcase.
Treatment: Exercise, fresh air, and tree-course meals.

Patient: Goldfish
Notes: Patient feels flushed.
Diagnosis: Doesn't get out enough. Thinks he sees giant faces.
Treatment: Needs to quit soaking.

Patient: Frog
Notes: Patient looks a little green, and his skin is clammy. Wart's up?
Diagnosis: This guy is about to croak.
Treatment: Needs more checkups, but there's a chance his check will bounce.

Patient: Pelican
Notes: Always puffin. Might be catching a bug.
Diagnosis: Flu?
Treatment: Uncertain, but it's going to be a big bill.

# WAITER! THERE'S A PTERODACTYL IN MY SOUP!

## Dinosaur Jokes

Bone up on these and you'll get mammoth laughs.

Who's the best-dressed dinosaur?
The Stegosaurus — he always looks sharp!

Why did the dinosaur go on Oprah?
He always wanted to be on a stalk show.

Why did the T-rex get a ticket?
He ran through a Stomp sign.

Caller: Can I speak to the Triceratops?
Secretary: Sorry, he's swamped right now.

What did the dinosaur tell his wife?
"I want to wear the plants in the family."

What's a dinosaur's favorite phone service?
Call wading.

What do you call a pterodactyl who complains?
A whine-o-saur.

What does a dinosaur put on his letters?
Stomps.

How do you tell a dinosaur from a pickle?
Try lifting it. If you can't get it off the floor, it's probably a dinosaur. But it might be a heavy pickle.

Why do girl dinosaurs wear bikinis?
So you can tell them apart from boy dinosaurs.

What is the most dangerous thing for dinosaurs with long tails?
Getting them caught in subway doors!

Why does a dinosaur have cracks between his toes?
To carry his library card.

Why are meteors better than toilet paper?
It only took one to wipe out all the dinosaurs.

What's the difference between a dinosaur and an Oreo?
Have you ever tried dipping a dinosaur in milk?

How do you make a dinosaur fly?
First, you start with a three-foot zipper . . .

**Where do raptors like to meet for a hamburger?
At the dinersaur.**

# *HERD ANY GOOD ONES LATELY?*

## Elephant Jokes

Elephant jokes are really big right now. Fortunately, we have a large supply.

How can you tell if there's an elephant in your bed?
By the big "E" on his pajamas.

Why do elephants clip their toenails?
So their ballet slippers will fit.

How can you tell if an elephant is living in your house?
By the giant tube top in your closet.

What's big, gray, and drinks Slim-Fast?
An elephant on a diet.

How do you make an elephant laugh?
Tell him a rhinoceros joke.

What's the difference between elephants and Pop-Tarts?
You need a much bigger fork to get elephants out of your toaster.

How do you know if there's an elephant in your fridge?
Footprints in the butter.

Why did the elephant paint his toenails different colors?
So he could hide in a dish of M&M's®.
I don't believe that.
Have you ever seen an elephant in a dish of M&M's?
No!
See? It works!

What's big and gray and goes up and down, up and down?
An elephant bungee jumping.

What did the elephant rock star say into the microphone?
"Tusking, one, two, three . . ."

# HOW TO MAKE
# AN ELEPHANT SMOOTHIE

Ingredients

1 elephant*

2 rabbits (optional)

500 gallons of ice cream

Cut elephant into bite-size pieces. This should take about six weeks. Put in blender along with ice cream. This will serve 2,000 people. If more are expected, two rabbits may be added, but use sparingly because most people do not like to find a hare in their drink.

*Warning: Children under 12 should not put an elephant into the blender unless assisted by an adult.

Why are elephants always wrinkled?
Have you ever tried to iron one?

What's the difference between an elephant and a canary?
They're both yellow, except for the elephant.

**Why do elephants have short tails?
So they don't trip when they skateboard.**

Why were the elephants kicked off the beach?
They were walking around with their trunks down.

How do you know if there's an elephant in your peanut butter?
Read the list of ingredients.

First elephant: Do you like my new dress? I got it for a crazy price!
Second elephant: You mean you got it for an absurd figure?

Why don't elephants eat rice pudding?
Because the raisins get stuck in their noses.

# YOU KNOW YOUR DOG

Tick baths involve incense and candles.

You need a chef to hide his worm pills.

Every day he gets his coat brushed.

# is **SPOILED** when . . .

He insists on XXL bones.

He'll dig holes, but won't get his paws dirty.

You're the one who sleeps in a cardboard box.

# HAVE YOU

a toilet bowl?

a bellhop?

a ski jump?

a home run?

a bacon strip?

a fruit punch?

a chopping block?

# EVER SEEN . . .

a salad dressing?

a flower shop?

a strawberry shake?

a catfish?

EEEEEEK!!

an ice cream?

a square dance?

a banana split?

# THIS PLACE IS BUGGED

## Creepy Crawly and Insect Jokes

These jokes are really fly. If you don't like them, buzz off.

What do snakes study in school?
Reading, writhing, and arithmetic.

What do you say to a spider at McDonald's?
"Would you like flies with that?"

What does a mongoose order at an ice-cream parlor?
A chocolate milk snake.

What do you call insects that are close friends?
Best bugs.

What do you serve a thirsty snake?
Cobra-Cola.

What do salamanders watch at night?
The evening newts.

What happened to the two bedbugs that fell in love?
They got married in the spring.

What's a tarantula's motto?
"Eat, drink, and be hairy."

Did you hear about the silkworms that ran a race?
They ended up in a tie.

What did the bee say to the flower?
"Hey, bud, when do you open?"

How can you tell when a bee is on the phone?
You get a buzzy signal.

How did the flea get to school?
He itchhiked.

Why did the moth eat the rug at the hotel?
It wanted to see the floor show.

What did one firefly say to another?
"You glow, girl!"

Where do fleas hang out after dinner?
On the front pooch.

Why did the termite put on pajamas?
He was going to a lumber party.

What kind of gum do snakes chew?
Wiggly Spearmint.

Why did the mosquito join a rock band?
To be the lead stinger.

**What do cobras like best
about going to the movies?
The snake previews.**

**Why did the personal trainer put spiders on the treadmill?**
**He had a few bugs to work out.**

How did the earthworm do in school?
He's at the bottom of his class.

Why is a caterpillar able to wait patiently
in her cocoon?
Because she knows she'll be out in a moth or so.

What kind of towels do snakes have?
Hiss and hers.

Did you hear about the snail that got beat up by two slugs? He went to the police and they asked him, "Did you get a look at the slugs who did this?"

He said, "No, it all happened so fast!"

One day a guy answers his door and finds a snail at his doorstep. The guy picks it up and tosses it into the garden. Two years later, he hears a knock on his door. He opens the door and finds the same snail. The snail says, "Hey, what was that all about?"

Knock knock.
Who's there?
Worm.
Worm who?
Worm in here, isn't it?

Knock knock.
Who's there?
Roach.
Roach who?
Roach you a letter — why didn't you write back?

**Why did the rock band hire a bunch of snakes?**
**They needed a worm-up band.**

# TEN THINGS YOU'LL NEVER HEAR PARENTS SAY

1. "We think you need to improve your Road Rage score."
2. "Maple syrup balloons? Cool!"
3. "Why not just drink it straight from the milk carton?"
4. "Bedtime? Not 'til you've read two comic books and watched some pro wrestling!"
5. "Great rap song. Turn it louder so we all can hear!"
6. "Why don't you control the remote? You have better taste than your sister!"
7. "Stick your arms out of the car window—there's a breeze!"
8. "Okay, but don't let homework cut into your TV time."
9. "No point in making the bed when you'll just have to unmake it again tonight."
10. "No, we're not there yet, but please — KEEP ASKING!"

# GO AHEAD AND I'LL KETCHUP

## Food Jokes

This section is stuffed with tasteless jokes. Dig in.

Bill: I know a man who lives on garlic alone.
Phil: No wonder he lives alone.

Teacher: What's our gross national product?
Student: Broccoli?

Why couldn't the sweet potato marry the TV reporter?
Because he was just a common tater.

What do you call cheese that isn't yours?
Nacho cheese.

What vegetables do you find in boats?
Leeks.

Why did the farmer drive across his field with a steamroller?
He wanted to grow mashed potatoes.

How do you honor an outstanding piece of bread?
You toast it!

Why did the teacher pass the mustard?
It knew all the right answers.

**Why don't rock bands ever go hungry?**
**They all have a pair of drumsticks.**

Why couldn't the janitor eat his lunch?
Because he forgot his lunch bucket.

What did the cook say to the salad?
"You're old enough to dress yourself."

Why didn't the cucumber want to become a pickle?
It was too jarring.

How do you keep bagels from being stolen?
Put lox on them.

Who is the leader of the popcorn?
The kernel.

How do you fix a broken pizza?
With tomato paste.

What did the grape say when it got squished?
Nothing, it just let out a little wine.

If a carrot and a lettuce ran a race, which would win?
The lettuce, because it's a head.

## FAMOUS FOODS

Okra Winfrey

Jennifer Cantelopez

Al Cappuccino

Broccoli Spears

Brad Cherry Pitt

Jude Slaw

Steven Spielburger

John Lemon

Elvis Parsley

Attila the Bun

When can you learn something at lunch?
When it's a three-course meal.


Did you hear about the pizza that made a movie?
It was panned.


Why did the pork cut go to school?
He had a lot to loin.


Why did the lazy guy visit a bakery?
So he could loaf around all day.


Did you hear about the man who married his silverware?
Now they're man and knife.


What does a clock do when it's hungry?
It goes back four seconds.


What kind of music do eggs like?
Yolk music.


Why did the egg go to Hollywood?
It was looking for its big break.


What's the happiest dessert?
Cheery pie.


Angry customer: Waiter, just look at this chicken. It's nothing
but skin and bones.
Waiter: What did you expect — feathers?

Customer: This food isn't fit for a pig!
Waiter: Just a minute, madam, I'll try to get some that is.

What's brown, wrinkled, and lives in a tower?
The Lunch Bag of Notre Dame.

What do you do when you see two pretzels fighting?
Straighten things out.

## What's orange and jumps out of airplanes?
## Carrot troopers.

# TOP TEN
# LEAST POPULAR
# BREAKFAST CEREALS

1. Fish 'n' Fiber
2. Broccoli Chex
3. Candy-Coated Cauliflower Crisps
4. Fruity Styrofoam Crunch
5. Li'l Bits o' Lint
6. Toasted Hairballs
7. Anchovy-O's
8. Frosted Mini-Beets
9. Flounder Puffs
10. Special P

Why did the baby cookie cry?
Because her mother was a wafer so long.

Did you hear about the restaurant on the moon?
The food is great, but there's no atmosphere.

What do you say to someone robbing a bakery?
"You take the cake."

What do aliens roast over a campfire?
Martian-mallows.

What did one lettuce say to another?
"You should have your head examined."

What do cucumbers do on vacation?
Veg out.

What happened when the pancake chef got mad?
He blew his stack.

How do you torture a lemon?
Give him a wedgie.

What do little grape preserves wear at bedtime?
Their jammies.

At the dance, what did the onion say to the carrot?
"Turnip the music."

What did one pretzel say to another?
"I've never been so insalted!"

What do bananas wear on their feet?
Slippers.

What happens when lollipops fight?
They get licked.

Where do you put a burglar who robbed a candy store?
Behind chocolate bars.

What does a carrot do when he needs a ride?
He calls a cabbage.

What do young beans do for fun?
They join the Boy Sprouts.

What did Mary order at the restaurant?
Mary had a little lamb.

What did one plate say to another?
"Lunch is on me!"

Why do potatoes make good detectives?
Because they keep their eyes peeled.

# A REAL NUTCASE

Why did the peanut cross the road?
To get to the shell station.

What does a nut say when it sneezes?
"Cashew."

What happens when nuts star in movies?
They get mixed reviews.

Did you hear about the peanuts walking down the street?
One was a salted.

# TOP TEN ICE CREAM FLAVORS REJECTED BY BASKIN ROBBINS

1. Celery Sorbet
2. Beet 'n' Broccoli Rhumba
3. Sushi Fudge Swirl
4. Cookies 'n' Clams
5. Sludge Brownie
6. Chocolate Almond Dirt
7. Pineapple Wood Chip
8. Dismember–Mint
9. Fudge Judy
10. Chunky Skunky

What TV show features bad bread slices?
*America's Toast Wanted.*

"I had a terrible night. I dreamed I ate a fifty-pound marshmallow."
"So what's so terrible about that?"
"When I woke up, my pillow was gone."

"Young man, there were two brownies in the pantry last night, and this morning there is only one. How do you explain that?"
"It was so dark I guess I missed it."

# DRESSED TO GRILL

Why didn't the hot dog star in movies?
He wasn't getting good rolls.

Why did the girl toss a hamburger at her friend?
She wanted to throw him a surprise patty.

How do they stop crime at McDonald's?
With a burger alarm.

What did one hot dog say to another?
"Hi, Frank."

Why did the hot dog win the race?
Because he was the wiener!

How do you kill a hamburger?
Smother it in onions.

Why did the hamburger
go to the gym?

It wanted better buns.

What's the difference between the jungle and a deli?
The jungle has a man-eating tiger, the deli has a man eating salami.

A mushroom said to his friends, "Let's have a party at my place!"
The carrot said, "What's the occasion?"
The mushroom shrugged. "'Cause I'm a fungi."

In the school cafeteria, the principal asked, "Any complaints?"
"Yes," said Justin. "The peas are hard as rocks."
The principal reached over with a fork and picked up some peas from Justin's plate. "They seem soft enough to me," he said, putting one in his mouth.
"I should hope so!" said Justin. "I've been chewing them for the last ten minutes."

Knock knock.
Who's there?
Butter.
Butter who?
Butter open the door, or else!

Knock knock.
Who's there?
Tacos.
Tacos who?
Tacos cheap!

Knock knock.
Who's there?
Lettuce.
Lettuce who?
Lettuce in, why don't you?

# WAITER, THERE'S A FLY IN MY SOUP!

## Serve Up Some Spicy Responses
## to the Classic Complaint . . .

"Sorry, sir, I forgot you wanted to dine alone."

"Don't worry — we won't charge extra."

"It's all right — he doesn't eat too much."

"Why are you complaining? He's the one who's dead!"

"Hmmm . . . there were two of them when I left the kitchen!"

"Shhhhh! The other customers will want one, too."

"Wait 'til you see what we put in the salad!"

"Don't worry, there's a spider on the bread."

Knock knock.
Who's there?
Donut.
Donut who?
Donut come near me — I'm sneezing!


Knock knock.
Who's there?
Frankfurter.
Frankfurter who?
Frankfurter lovely evening.


Knock knock.
Who's there?
Omelet.
Omelet who?
Omelet smarter than I look!


Knock knock.
Who's there?
Celery.
Celery who?
Celery dance?


Knock knock.
Who's there?
Artichoke.
Artichoke who?
Artichokes when they serve meatloaf for lunch!


Knock knock.
Who's there?
Turnip.
Turnip who?
Turnip the heat — I'm freezing!

Knock knock.
Who's there?
Muffin.
Muffin who?
Muffin ventured, muffin gained.


Knock knock.
Who's there?
Sushi.
Sushi who?
Sushi told me to look you up!


Knock knock.
Who's there?
Quiche.
Quiche who?
Quiche me, you fool!


Knock knock.
Who's there?
Olive.
Olive who?
Olive these food jokes are pretty lousy.

# ONE MORNING AT BREAKFAST

# YOU KNOW IT'S TIME to give up

You're out of pepperoni? No problem!

Your favorite pets are gummy animals.

You try to scramble chocolate Easter eggs.

# CANDY when . . .

Your clothes are 100% cotton...candy.

You see your dentist more than your dad.

The only vegetable you eat is candy corn.

# TABLE TALK

# "YOUR BROTHER IS SO STUPID . . ."

## A Snaptitude Test

**Can you "bust" a good snap? Fill in the blanks to see how good you are at insults.**

**1. Your neighbor is so FAT . . .**
a) she went to a buffet and got a group discount.
b) when she looks at a menu, she says "okay."
c) they had to let out the shower curtain.
d) _____.

**2. Your brother is so STUPID . . .**
a) he trips over the cordless phone.
b) he went to a drive-in to see "Closed for Winter."
c) he couldn't get vanity license plates, so he changed his name to LMZ7243.
d) _____.

**3. Your cousin is so UGLY . . .**
a) her dentist treats her by mail.
b) all the neighbors chipped in for curtains.
c) people dress up as her for Halloween.
d) _____.

**4. Your lab partner is so SKINNY . . .**
a) she hula hoops with a LifeSaver.
b) she naps in a pencil case.
c) she bungee jumps with dental floss.
d) _____.

**5. Your best friend is so SHORT . . .**
a) he can't see over the shag rug.
b) I have socks taller than him.
c) his boxer shorts drag on the ground.
d) _____.

**6. Your math teacher is so OLD . . .**
a) she has a picture of Moses in her yearbook.
b) she knew Burger King when he was a prince.
c) she was shown on *Antiques Roadshow.*
d) _____.

**7. Your school is so POOR . . .**
a) the lunchroom washes paper plates.
b) the principal steals your lunch money.
c) instead of computers, each kid gets an Etch-a-Sketch.
d) _____.

**8. This book is so STUPID . . .**
a) it isn't worth the toilet paper it's printed on.
b) it thinks Cheez Whiz is for geniuses.
c) it makes *99½ Gross Jokes* look like *The Collected Works of William Shakespeare.*
d) _____.

**SCORING:**
For every (a) answer, give yourself three points. For every (b) answer, give yourself two points. For every (c) answer, give yourself one point. For every (d) answer, give yourself a wedgie.

**WHAT IT MEANS:**

1 point: The only snaps you bust are on blue jeans. You need to get out and diss more.

6–10 points: You're a wise-cracking master snapper who puts the "I" in insult. Hope you like getting your butt kicked!

# GO TO YOUR TOMB!

## Scary, Creepy Monster Jokes

Tell these jokes and you'll be the after-life of the party.

What does the Blob say on his answering machine?
"Leave a message at the sound of the creep."

Why did the vampire excuse himself?
He had to go to the bat room.

How do witches stay in touch?
By spell phone.

What kind of television set does Godzilla have?
A big-scream TV.

What's a witch's favorite magazine?
*Warts Illustrated.*

What kind of car does Dracula drive?
A Necks-us.

What kind of music do ghosts like best?
Rhythm 'n' boos.

What do vampires do in the fall?
Their bat-to-school shopping!

What do mummies like best about football?
The postgame wrap-up.

How do ghosts keep their babies safe in the car?
They put them in car sheets.

What does Frankenstein say at a rap concert?
"I'd like to give a shout-out to my creeps."

What's Dracula's favorite part of the airplane ride?
The in-fright movie.

When did Frankenstein cross the street?
When the sign read, STALK.

What do zombies watch on MTV?
*Total Request Dead.*

What does a witch order when she stays in a hotel?
Broom service.

What kind of jokes do vampires tell?
Neck-neck jokes.


Why did the ghost go to the newsstand?
He wanted chains for a dollar.


How do witches like their cheeseburgers?
Medium-scared.


Why don't comedians perform for ghosts?
They boo!


What do you call a ghost who haunts Congress?
Shrieker of the House.


**Why did the ghouls join a picket line?**
**They heard there was a demon-stration.**

Why didn't the zombie go to school?
He was feeling rotten.

Why did King Kong climb the Empire State Building?
He didn't fit in the elevator.

How does Godzilla do aerobics?
On the Stairmonster.

What does a mummy take for a cold?
Coffin drops.

What do you give the Blob when he misbehaves?
A slime-out.

How do werewolves sign their holiday cards?
Best vicious.

What kind of truck does Godzilla drive?
A monster truck.

What sport do mummies like best?
Casketball.

Why was Godzilla arrested for throwing a party?
He threw it across the Grand Canyon.

Why are teenage girl mummies annoying?
They spend too much time in the bath tomb.

Why did the witch take her broom to bed?
It was time to go to sweep.

Why couldn't the witch get into the show?
It was standing broom only.

Why was the ghost rushed to the hospital?
To have his ghoul bladder removed.

What do you do when a werewolf comes to school?
Make him howl monitor.

What's the first thing Frankenstein reads in the newspaper?
His horror-scope.

# TOP TEN CREEPY TV SHOWS

1. *Lifestyles of the Witch and Famous*
2. *NYPD Boo*
3. *Good Moaning America*
4. *Fiends*
5. *Claw & Order*
6. *Maul My Children*
7. *Saturday Night Dead*
8. *Eyewitness Ooz*
9. *Baywitch*
10. *Wide Underworld of Sports*

How did the ghost teacher explain the lesson on walking through walls?
She went through it again and again.

Why did the boy monster kiss the girl monster on the back of the neck?
That's where her lips were.

Why couldn't the mummy come to the telephone?
Because he was tied up.

Spook #1: How was the party at the cemetery?
Spook #2: The place was dead!

How did the witch get to the second floor?
She took the scarecase.

What do gourmet witches serve?
Twelve-curse meals.

What did the ticket taker for the pyramids say?
"Satisfaction guaranteed or your mummy back!"

What does a monster call a jogger?
Fast food.

What did the Invisible Man's mother say to him?
"We never see you anymore!"

What does every celebrity ghoul want to be?
The ghost of *Saturday Night Live*.

What did Dracula say to his new assistant?
"We can use some new blood around here!"

How did Godzilla like swallowing Big Ben?
He found it time-consuming.

Why did Godzilla eat almost an entire hotel, except the top three floors?
His doctor wanted him to cut down on suites.

A vampire took a vacation on a cruise ship. The headwaiter asked if he'd like to check out their menu. "No thanks," said the vampire. "But do you have a passenger list?"

A zombie went to pick up his girlfriend to take her to the senior prom. Her mother came to the door and said, "Beth can't go to the prom tonight because she's got the flu."
He met his zombie friends at the graveyard. "Okay," he said. "Can anyone help me dig up another date?"

How does one monster greet another monster that has green skin with six bulging eyes dripping with pus, five running noses, and is drooling yellow ooze from its three mouths? "Hey, handsome!"

Mother monster: Do you think we should take Junior to the zoo?
Father monster: No, dear. If the zoo wants him they'll just have to come get him.

Knock knock.
Who's there?
Hairy.
Hairy who?
Hairy up, I haven't got all day!

Knock knock.
Who's there?
Weird.
Weird who?
Weird you get such a hideous face?

—

Knock knock.
Who's there?
Crypt.
Crypt who?
Crypt up from behind to scare you!


Knock knock.
Who's there?
Goblin.
Goblin who?
Goblin food will make you sick!


Knock knock.
Who's there?
Howl.
Howl who?
Howl I get in if you don't open the door?


Knock knock.
Who's there?
Werewolf.
Werewolf who?
Werewolf I be without you?

# IF MONSTERS GOT REPORT CARDS

We dug up some school records at Frankenstein Junior High, where there's some pretty stiff competition . . .

## REPORT CARD

STUDENT: DRACULA
SUCKING: C
BITING: D-
COMMENTS: Has a bat attitude. Always hanging around after class. He's suspended!

## REPORT CARD

STUDENT: THE INVISIBLE MAN
LURKING: B
CREEPING: C-
COMMENTS: Is frequently absent. Has many friends, but I don't know what they see in him.

## REPORT CARD

STUDENT: KING TUT
SLEEPING: C
UNWINDING: D+
COMMENTS: His work really sphinx. Very wrapped up in himself. Always asking for his mummy.

## REPORT CARD

STUDENT: FRANKENSTEIN
SCIENCE: C-
BODYBUILDING: B+
COMMENTS: Can't seem to pull himself together. Borrows other students' brains and doesn't return them.

## REPORT CARD

STUDENT: CYCLOPS
STARING: D+
GLARING: B-
COMMENTS: This is one lousy pupil. Will never make it through Junior Eye School.

## REPORT CARD

STUDENT: ZACHARY ZOMBIE
DECOMPOSITION WRITING: A
ROTTING: B+
COMMENTS: Buries himself in his studies, but his work is rotten. Needs to get a life.

## REPORT CARD

STUDENT: WANDA THE WITCH
FLYING: A
SPELLING: B-
COMMENTS: At lunch, complains about small potions. Often falls behind in cursework. Might be happier at an all-ghoul's school.

## REPORT CARD

STUDENT: THE BLOB
OOZING: B+
REVOLTING: A
COMMENTS: Everything goes in one ear and out the others. Can't keep his mouths shut.

## REPORT CARD

STUDENT: GARY THE GHOST
HAUNTING: B-
PUBLIC SHRIEKING: A
COMMENTS: Won't stay in his sheet. When it's time to do classroom chores, he disappears.

## REPORT CARD

STUDENT: NELLY THE SKELETON
RATTLING: C
SHAKING: A-
COMMENTS: Doesn't have any body to hang around with. Needs to bone up on his studies.

## REPORT CARD

STUDENT: GODZILLA
DESTROYING: B+
DEMOLISHING: A-
COMMENTS: Keeps stepping on the school, which is very disruptive.

## REPORT CARD

STUDENT: SWAMP THING
SCREAMING: B
SCREECHING: A-
COMMENTS: Always getting bogged down in his work.

## REPORT CARD

STUDENT: THE HEADLESS HORSEMAN
GRADE: INCOMPLETE

# TOP TEN SIGNS YOUR TEACHER IS A WEREWOLF

1. Drinks from the faculty toilet
2. Always styling her back hair
3. Sometimes comes to work without her face combed
4. Howls when she hears a good joke
5. Trims her elbows during homeroom
6. Admits she does some "moonlighting"
7. Sheds all over the teachers' lounge
8. Wears a fur coat even in summer
9. Slobbers over your homework
10. When you shake her hand, you get rug burn

# HOW'S BUSINESS?

Find the quote that best matches the workers listed below. We've done the first one for you.

The correct description for number 1, toupee salesman, is letter K.

1. Toupee salesman

2. Cannon manufacturer

3. Scuba diver

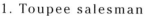

4. Oil driller

5. Watch repairman

6. Origami instructor

7. Weather forecaster

8. Donut baker

10. Elevator operator

9. Gardener

11. Lamp salesman

12. Archaeologist

13. Trapeze artist

14. Cemetery worker

15. Aerobics teacher

16. Circus fat man

QUOTE:
A. "I'm in over my head."
B. "Boring."
C. "Expanding."
D. "I'm getting the hang of it."
E. "Times are tough."
F. "Right now there's some high pressure."
G. "Mine is growing."
H. "It has its ups and downs."
I. "My career is in ruins."
J. "It's working out."
K. "Lately it's been falling off."
L. "It's booming!"
M. "I'm tired of the hole business."
N. "Pretty soon I'll have to fold."
O. "The future is bright."
P. "I'm digging it."

# URINE TROUBLE NOW!

## Gross Jokes

We collected so many bathroom jokes, we're wiped out.
Warning: Most of them stink.

Why did the toilet paper feel good?
He was on a roll.

What kind of book does a dirty sock write?
A best smeller.

What's more disgusting, smelly socks or a short supermarket worker?
The short guy, 'cause he's a little grocer.

What's green and red and goes 50 miles per hour?
A frog in a blender.

Mother: What are you doing with that saw around your little brother?
Son: Well, he's my half-brother now.

What do you say to a one-legged hitchhiker?
"Hop in."

What did one eye say to the other?
"Between us, something smells."

**Why did the boy bring a trash bag to the movies?**
**Because his mom said, "Take out the garbage!"**

# TOP TEN FUNNIEST TOWNS THAT REALLY EXIST (WE SWEAR!)

1. Flush, Kansas
2. Riddle, Wyoming
3. Toad Suck, Arkansas
4. Gas City, Indiana
5. Tightwad, Missouri
6. Boogertown, North Carolina
7. Pimple Hill, Pennsylania
8. Go Home, Canada
9. Ding Dong, Texas
10. Poop Creek, Oregon

What's the last thing that goes through a bug's mind when it hits the windshield?
Its feet.

Phil: Where are you taking that skunk?
Bill: To the gym.
Phil: What about the smell?
Bill: Oh, he'll get used to it.

A kid walked into his house with a handful of dog droppings and says to his mother, "Look what I almost stepped in!"

What's the difference between boogers and beets?
Kids won't eat beets.


Why does Piglet smell so bad?
He plays with Pooh.


What do you do if you find a ferret in your bathroom?
Wait until he's finished.


When a guy with acne goes to jail, what happens?
He breaks out.


Why did the toilet paper roll down the hill?
It wanted to get to the bottom.


Did you hear about the man who was arrested for peeing in a wheat field?
He was going against the grain.


Why did the mother throw her baby down the stairs?
She wanted to see him take his first twenty steps!


Mother: What's your little brother yelling about?
Linda: I let him lick the beater after I made cookies.
Mother: So?
Linda: I should have turned it off first.

# WHAT DO YOU CALL . . . ?

What do you call a dog with no legs under your car?

Jack

What do you call a boy flying over a fence?

Homer

What do you call a girl caught on a fence?

Barb

What do you call a boy on a butter plate?

Pat

What do you call a girl with a coat on her head?

Peg

What do you call a girl at the beach?

Sandy

What do you call a boy in a pile of leaves?

Russell

What do you call a girl on a barbecue grill?

Patty

What do you call a boy on a grill?

Frank

What do you call two men hanging on the side of a window?

Curt and Rod

What do you call a boy with a shovel?

Doug

What do you call a girl with one leg shorter than the other?

Eileen

# SHOW 'N' SMELL

THESE PHRASES ARE A GAS.

Whoever smelt it dealt it.

Whoever denied it supplied it.

Whoever accuses blew the fuses.

Whoever rebuts it cuts it.

What's the best time to use the toilet?
In the wee-wee hours of the morning.

What did the toilet say to the sink?
I'm feeling a little flushed.

How do you make a maggot stew?
Keep him waiting for a couple of hours.

**What did the nose say to the ear?
"Gotta run!"**

Molly: I've been going out with my boyfriend for two weeks and just found out he has a wooden leg. What should I do?
Polly: Break it off.

What did the dirt say to the rain?
"Thanks to you, my name is mud."

# 10. TOP TEN MOVIES NOW PLAYING AT THE DISGUSTING CINEPLEX 10.

1. *Lard of the Rings*
2. *Star Warts*
3. *Scoobie Doo Doo*
4. *The Sound of Mucus*
5. *The Pukémon Movie*
6. *Wizard of Ooze*
7. *Mold Mountain*
8. *Roadkill Bill*
9. *Honey, I Stunk the Kids*
10. *James and the Giant Leech*

Did you hear the one about the foot fungus?
It grows on you.

Did you hear the one about the old bag of potato chips?
It's pretty stale.

Did you hear the one about the vomiting giant?
It's all over town.

# TOP TEN
## GROSS TV SHOWS

1. *Behind the Mucus*
2. *Saturday Night Lice*
3. *Antiques Moldshow*
4. *Maul My Children*
5. *Will and Grease*
6. *CBS Eyewitness Ooze*
7. *NYPD Goo*
8. *Socks in the City*
9. *The Slopranos*
10. *The Pimple Life*

Why didn't the nose make the softball team?
Nobody picked him!

Why is basketball a disgusting sport?
Because the players dribble.

What do you call someone who puts her right hand into the mouth of a giant shark?
Lefty.

What else is disgusting about basketball?
The players throw up.

What's the difference between a pair of smelly socks and a school lunch?
In an emergency, you could always eat the socks!

**Remember when I vomited my school lunch? Let's not bring that up again!**

# TOP TEN THINGS OVERHEARD AT A CANNIBAL FAMILY BARBECUE

1. "Let's invite the neighbors for lunch."
2. "Get dressed — we're having company."
3. "Mom sure makes a great hamburger."
4. "I'd like to toast our guest of honor!"
5. "My stomach hurts. I think I ate someone who disagreed with me."
6. "Want to try out the hot tub?"
7. "Lately, I'm fed up with people."
8. "I told you not to speak with someone in your mouth!"
9. "Don't get into a stew!"
10. "How did your team do today, son?" "We creamed them."

Where do you shop if you're a one-armed man?
At the secondhand store.

Why did Ozzy Osbourne lose his job at the candy store?
He kept biting the heads off chocolate bunnies.

What did the teacher say as his glass eye rolled down the drain?
"Guess I've lost another pupil!"

What did the surgeon say as he sewed up the patient?
"That's enough out of you!"

Why didn't the corpse visit friends when he started to decompose?
He felt like he was losing face.

Why did the cannibal go to a heavy metal concert?
He needed more iron in his diet.

A guy ordered a bowl of spaghetti at a restaurant. The waiter said, "The guy next to you got the last plate."
He looks over and sees the guy's plate of spaghetti is full. He says, "If you're not going to eat it, may I have some?"
The other guy says, "No, help yourself." He starts to eat it and about halfway down, his fork gets caught on something. It's a dead rat, and he vomits the spaghetti back onto the plate.
The other guy says, "That's about as far as I got, too."

A man lost an ear in an accident at work and asked his friend to help him look for it. They searched for an hour, and finally his friend found the ear.
"That's not mine," said the man. "Mine had a pencil behind it."

Two cockroaches were crawling around in a garbage can. One said to the other, "Did you hear about the new restaurant across the street? It's got a new refrigerator, the kitchen floor is spotless, and all the shelves are clean." The other cockroach grimaced and said, "Do you mind? Not while I'm eating!"

Knock knock.
Who's there?
Ooze.
Ooze who?
Ooze going to change my diaper?


Knock knock.
Who's there?
European.
European who?
European in my bathroom and I need to use it!

# TODAY AT THE CANNIBAL CAFETERIA

## SCHOOL LUNCH MENU
## ALL STUDENTS WILL BE SERVED

Sloppy Joe seasoned with Rosemary

Frank and Beans

Hamburger Patty

Big Mac

Chicken Fingers served on lazy Susan

Chef Salad

Shishke Bob

Pretzel Rod

Choice of Eskimo Pie, Apple Betty, or a Brownie

Students must remove their trays when everyone's eaten.

# YOU KNOW YOU are

You can get dressed without getting out of bed.

Instead of reading the lunch menu, people look at your shirt.

At graduation, the principal throws you your diploma.

# a SLOB when...

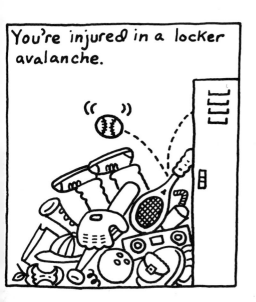

You're injured in a locker avalanche.

To find your little brother, you listen for tapping sounds.

You finally find the remote.

# JOKE-O-MATIC

If you think you can do better than me, make up your own #$%*&@ jokes!

1. **What's _____ and goes round and round?**
   (color)
   *A _____stuck in a revolving door.*
   (vegetable that's the same color)

2. **How do you make a _____ shake?**
   (disgusting insect)
   *Take it to a scary movie.*

3. **How do you make a _____ float?**
   (large animal)
   *Take a dish of ice cream and add two scoops of _____.*
   (same animal)

4. **What's the best way to talk to a _____?**
   (scary animal)
   *Long distance.*

5. **How do you stop a _____-pound _____ from charging?**
   (huge number)    (big animal)
   *Take away his credit cards.*

**6. How do you catch a runaway _____?**
(funny animal)
*Hide behind a tree and make a noise like a _____.*
(animal's fave food)


**7. What's the difference between a _____ and a**
(large animal)
_____?
(tiny object)
*If you don't know, I'm not sending you to the store!*


**8. What do _____s have that no other animal has?**
(animal)
*Baby _____s.*
(same animal)


**9. What time is it when a _____ sits on your _____?**
(large animal)                    (vehicle)
*Time to get a new _____.*
(same vehicle)


**10. What's _____ and a mile and a half high?**
(color)
*The Empire State _____.*
(vegetable that's the same color)

# YOU KNOW YOUR DOG

He has a two-shoe-a-day habit.

His belly is rubbed by a licensed masseuse.

He gets another dog to do his fetching.

# is **SPOILED** when . . .

He invites friends over for drinks.

He talks on his cell bone nonstop.

He refuses to eat your homework.

# TOP TEN
# OTHER USES FOR
# THIS BOOK

1. Cover it with the book jacket of *Advanced Calculus* to impress people.
2. Handy toupee rest for vice-principal
3. One word: origami
4. Hollow out inside for hiding Cheetos.
5. Yoga mat for Barbie
6. Perfect drain stopper for the Jacuzzi
7. Great for swatting killer flies
8. Wear under your shirt to shield against death rays.
9. One book = 72 paper airplanes.
10. Change letters to "This Book Is a Coke." Leave on soda machine.

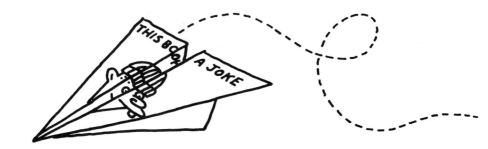

Look for
THIS BOOK IS
A JOKE
2
Coming
Soon!